# Mānoa Stream

# Mānoa Stream

Ann Inoshita

Kahuaomānoa Press
Honolulu, Hawaiʻi

*~Kahuaomānoa Press~*

| | |
|---|---|
| President & Chief Editor | Brandy Nālani McDougall |
| Vice-President & Managing Editor | Ann Inoshita |
| Associate Editor & Treasurer | Ryan Oishi |
| Assistant Editors | Kai Gaspar, Bryan Kamaoli Kuwada |
| Typesetting & Book Design | Brent Fujinaka |

Cover photgraph by Ann Inoshita.

Kahuaomānoa means, in ʻōlelo Hawaiʻi, "the fruit of Mānoa"
and "foundation of Mānoa."

Kahuaomānoa Press is dedicated toward the publication and promotion
of excellence in student art and literature. As such, every effort is made
to privilege the student voice and perspective first and foremost.

This book contains poems of fiction. For some poems, the author has chosen
the first person as a way to present the poem. Some poems may have been
modified since their original publication.

# Acknowledgments

Special thanks to the following people:

Kahuaomānoa Press for publishing student work. Brandy Nālani McDougall for kindness, experience, and leadership. Kai Gaspar, Kuʻualoha Hoʻomanawanui, Bryan Kamaoli Kuwada, and Ryan Oishi for support and advice from editing to book launch. Brent Fujinaka for all your assistance.

Thank you everyone who helped publish my first book of poems. Robert Sullivan for honesty and guidance. Marie Hara for the talks, encouragement, and enthusiasm. Juliet S. Kono for the kind words. Kent Sakoda fo talking about da Pidgin. Joy Kobayashi-Cintrón for feedback. Puna Lee Nouchi and Celeste Matsukawa for advice.

Appreciation to Eric Chock and Darrell H. Y. Lum, Editors of *Bamboo Ridge*, Patrice M. Wilson, Editor of *Hawaiʻi Pacific Review*, Susan Schultz, Editor of *Tinfish*, and Tim Denevi, Editor of *vice-versa*.

Special thanks to the English Department and Cristina Bacchilega at the University of Hawaiʻi at Mānoa. Thank you Morgan Blair, Albert Wendt, Anne Kennedy, Rodney Morales, and Ian MacMillan for all your assistance.

My deepest gratitude to The John Young Foundation and Debbie Young. Thank you for your generosity, understanding, and for helping so many students.

Appreciation to the Student Activity and Program Fee Board and the Campus Center Board Activities Council for supporting readings.

Bachan, Jichan, Mom, Dad, and Lynn for a solid foundation.

Mrs. Nora Saito for being supportive of me especially small kid time. Mrs. Daisy Ho who gave me confidence that being a poet is possible. Susan Fierro for clarity and friendship. Feng Feng Hutchins for all the talks about writing.

Thank you to all who supported me from the beginning.

Appreciation to the journals that originally printed these poems:

*Bamboo Ridge: Journal of Hawai'i Literature and Arts*
"Eternal Love," "Garbage," "Modest Inquisition,"
"Plumeria," "Repulsive Love," and "TV"

*Hawai'i Pacific Review*
"Mortality"

Forthcoming poems:

*Hawai'i Pacific Review Best of the Decade 1998-2007*
"Mortality"

*Tinfish*
"Ogo Picking"

*vice-versa*
"No Can Sleep," "On the Way Home," "Roses,"
"Stereotype," and "Zebra Dove"

# Contents

-Mortality-

-Outside-

# Foreword

"I love poetry...I like to write poems...I have many of them...I truly have something to say..." These are exclamations I have frequently heard from students in years of teaching. However, after looking at their poems, that something to say has often been abstract, riddled with cliché, or simply banal.

In addition, very few students who aspire to become poets can write a substantial number of poems, for "writing one or two decent poems does not a poet make," as someone once told me. In my experience, it is the gift of tenacity that sets apart those who wish to become poets from those who truly are. Furthermore, rare are the students who are able to release the singing in the body to resonate with words that spin in the mind, this over and beyond their ability to master the major concepts of poetry. Ann Inoshita is one such student who has been able to "release the singing" in the crafting of her poems. Her first book, *Mānoa Stream*, is a testament to her perseverance, her work having the attributes of a fresh, insightful, and emerging voice that is full of surprises in its language and meaning. As I often say to my students, writing a body of *good* poems is not for the incurious or for the faint of heart.

In the first two sections of her collection, *Mānoa Stream* and *Rememba Wen*, Ann creates unique vignettes written in Pidgin that illuminate the angst and difficulty of growing up in Hawai'i's clash of cultures—local, American, even ancestral—and it is especially difficult when one is *different* in a culture that does not appreciate someone who deviates from the norm. Thus, the skewed viewpoint of Ann's child protagonist is especially poignant, a viewpoint where the child looks up to adults to cue her as how to behave in a puzzling world. With this approach of childhood, we are brought back to our own misunderstandings of life and can laugh at them, unabashedly. Poems like "TV," "May Day Festival in Elementary School," "East Coast Trip: 1981," and "Japan Trip," have a bittersweet but endearing quality to them. In "Japan Trip," the narrator's plea is plaintive in her search for identity as a person caught in a whirlpool of different cultures. The sadness of having lost something of one's identity is deftly touched upon in the following lines:

Sometime hard for be Local.
Sometime hard for be American.
And sometime hard for be Japanese.

Sometime I feel like I no belong no place.
I wonda if people tink befo dey come stay Hawai'i.
Hawai'i good but I know I wen lose someting.
Hard for go back.

However, the underlying seriousness and sadness of the messages in some of her poems, especially those that carry a historical component, are not lost to the reader, as in "Reagan Wen Get Shot," "Pearl Harbor," and "Hiroshima." The poem "Hiroshima," for example, starts with "We wen visit da museum and had all kine pikchas on top da walls...but I remamba had one lady and her breast wen melt." Later, her sister who had seen these pictures with her gets an upset stomach and the child says:

I wonda if she was sick fo real.
You know she wen see all da pikchas
and hard fo see dat kine stuff.
Hard fo forget.
Maybe das why we wen go.

The reader is able to appreciate the irony of the whole poem with the last two lines "Hard fo forget. / Maybe das why we wen go." Ann sets it up in this manner because people need to be reminded of the horrors of such a disaster.

The poems move from childhood puzzlement, albeit in a relatively secure world because of supportive parents, to one of adolescent bewilderment seen in the negotiating and compromises made by the narrator as with the cruelty of classmates ("Intermediate School"), sexual harassment ("Dancing Wit One Molesta" and "Bumping on da Bus"), and her first kiss ("Prom Night"). Although some poems remain in Pidgin, most of the thematically metaphoric ones remain in Standard English; they gradually become adult in tone and execution, even unduly dark. The poems "Red Velvet Cake," and "Garbage" in the section called *Wen Nobody Stay Looking* fit this category. The next section she has entitled *Mortality,* continues with poems that are darker in nature, the poems dealing with love, death, and illness. The poems "Feva," "Modest Inquisition," "Plumeria," and "Eternal Love," are a departure from the earlier sections, nonetheless different, lovely and surprising in content.

To the reader's relief, her collection does not end pessimistically but on a hopeful note. It takes us back to safety with her last section called, *Outside,* where a semblance of normality is back in place with "Walks with Bachan," "Roses," and "Taking Pictures," with the last poem, "Zebra Dove" ending in five beautifully crafted lines:

The zebra dove trusts
and lives.

I close my eyes
wanting to dissolve
myself into everything.

I anticipate many more poems from Ann in the future, written in Pidgin as well in the mature voice that she has cultivated in this, her first collection. There is humor and depth to her work, a necessary combination to endure in the writing she has chosen to do. I look forward to reading more of her poems, for she has proven that she can write in a genre that is unforgiving to many who aspire to share in its glow.

She has a solid start.

*Juliet S. Kono*

For Bachan, Jichan, Mom, Dad, and Lynn.

Because of you, I know what it's like to be home.

~Mānoa Stream~

# TV

Going come dark so my madda call me
fo go back inside da house.
Can smell tonkatsu from da kitchen
and my madda turn on da TV.
"Dinner going be ready soon."

I watch TV and dey playing *Superman.*
"Mommy, one day I going save everybody.
I going be Superman."
She turn da tonkatsu ova in da pan
and tell me das one good idea.

Den, get one commercial about trips to Hawai'i.
"Mommy, one day we going Hawai'i."
She look at me funny kine.
I tell her as one good idea fo go Hawai'i.
Everybody can live in grass shacks
and going be good fun fo drink da kine
tropical drink wit da fruit and umbrella
and stay outside all da time.
She tell me we live Hawai'i.

I look at her.
"No, we no live Hawai'i.
We live in one house like everybody on da TV."
She tell me one mo time we live Hawai'i
and dinner going be ready pretty soon.
My madda dunno wat she talking about.
We no live Hawai'i.

Now, da TV playing one old movie.
My madda said as *Breakfast at Tiffany's*
and da lady da actress Audrey Hepburn.
Look like one nice lady.  I like her.

Get one wild party and dis guy wit small eyes
talking weird.  I no undastand wat he saying.
"Mommy, who dat guy?"

My madda no answer, and she move da katsu
on one plate.  She tell me dinner ready.

I eat and she tell me we going have
spaghetti tomorrow.  I like spaghetti.
"So who da guy wit da small eyes in da movie?
Da one dat talk funny."
She tell me she dunno who him,
but in da movie, he suppose to be one Oriental guy.
"Yeah?"
She wen nod and tell me fo eat.
"Wat Oriental?"
She look surprise.  "Us Oriental."
"I thought we Japanese?"
"We Japanese."

Afta she pau wash dishes,
she hold me close, and I can hear
her heart and her voice vibrate wen she talk.
Den, she stroke my hair, and I get sleepy.

My madda tink she know everyting,
but she dunno.
I not Oriental,
I no live Hawai'i,
and one day I going save everybody
just like Superman.

# Red Banana in da First Grade

My madda wen get red banana
from somebody yestaday,
so I going color my banana red
fo show da teacha dat I smart.

Da teacha wen walk by me fo see how I doing.
I smile showing her my pikcha.
Den she ask me if bananas are red.
I proudly tell her, "Yes."

Her face wen change right dea.
She wen look real mad and tell me,
"Bananas are not red.  Bananas are yellow."
I neva know wat fo say.

Afta school, I wen look fo da red banana at home,
but no mo.
Den my madda came home, and I ask her,
"Where da red banana?"

My madda said she wen give um to somebody.
I told her my teacha said no mo red banana
only get yellow kine.

My madda said da red kine fo cooking,
but she neva cook red banana befo.
I look at da empty table and ask my madda again,
"Get red banana, yeah?"

She wen smile and tell me,
"Of course, get red banana."
Den I show her my pikcha from school,
and she put da pepa on da ice box.

# May Day Festival in Elementary School

We was getting ready fo May Day and all da kids
wen bring flower from dea yard fo decorate da stage
fo da May Day king and queen.
I dunno if had dis kine celebration long time ago,
but we get now.

Da king, queen, and da court was from da six grade
and dey was watching all da classes do pleny dances fo dem.
My class had two groups and each group
suppose to have one different dance.
One dance was about all da nations of da world.
Da odda dance had someting fo do wit Disneyland.

I wen forget which group I was in,
and I neva like ask da teacha.
I suppose to rememba stuff laidat.
Sometime I go learn da nation of da world dance.
Odda kine time I go learn da Disneyland dance.
I wen go make two costume too.
I wen talk to da teachas about my kimono,
and I wen make one Mickey Mouse cap.

One day, one teacha wen ask me wat group I belong in.
I no answer. I dunno.
Den da teacha ask me wat group I like be in.
Was hard fo decide. I like be in da two.
Da teacha wait long time.
Den she no can wait any longa.
I wasting her time.

So da teacha wen put me in da nation of da world dance.
I dunno how come.
Maybe I already had one kimono and not everybody get one
and easy fo make one Mickey Mouse cap.
Anyways, I wore da kimono I had at home,
and I wen dance in front of everybody fo May Day.
Was good fun. I wish dey neva divide da class laidat but.
Mo betta if everybody wen dance da two dances.

# East Coast Trip: 1981

Our elementary school class stay learning about history
so we wen go on one east coast trip fo visit pleny states.
We climb da Statue of Liberty.
We look da Washington Monument.
We wen go any kine place.
I forget which state we was in
but we was all hungry
so we wen go inside one restaurant.
Everybody wen stare at us.
Maybe cuz we one tour group
or we all wearing big kine jackets as why.
Eh, we not used to da cold. We freezing.

Wen take long time fo get one seat
maybe dey tink we all like sit on one big table
but we no need one big table.
We only one tour group. Each family can sit separate.
Some people tired wait
so dey wen go across da street go McDonalds.
My fadda wen look at my madda.
Dey no talk, and we still stay waiting fo one table.
Wen we finally wen get one table, we pick wat we like eat.
We had to wait long time again fo somebody fo come get da orda.

My fadda wanted fo go but I wen like stay.
I like see wat kine food dey get ova hea
so my madda look my fadda and he wen sit down again.
I saw da waitas ask people who wen just come in wat dey like eat
and we neva even stay orda yet.
Finally, one waita come and he no smile. He act like he no like
    be hea.
He wen take our orda. Den take long time fo us fo get our food.
Everybody who wen go McDonalds pau eat already.
I wanted fo go too but da table so quiet. I neva like talk.
I wish I neva tell I wanted fo eat hea. We finally wen get da food
    so too late fo go.
Dey give us only little bit but. I look da odda tables, dey get pleny
    food.

I ask my madda how come we get little bit food, and she no talk.
She just say, "Mo betta we wen go McDonalds."
I wish I stay back home.  Not cold like ova hea.

## Reagan Wen Get Shot

We wen visit da Capitol building in Washington, D.C.
and Congressman Daniel Akaka wen greet us.
Nice fo see somebody local ova hea.

Den he tell us Reagan wen get shot
and everybody in da tour group was shock
cuz we neva know anyting laidis wen happen.

So we wen go back to da hotel and watch TV.
Dey was playing back da shooting.  Was all ova da pepa too.

Da President was coughing up blood,
and we was waiting fo hear how he was doing.
Funny kine feeling.

I told my madda I like go home already.
I no like stay hea no mo.
My madda hug me and tell me no worry.

My fadda told me da President going be ok.
Dat dis all going be part of history
and I going learn mo about our country.
I told him I rather read one book.
I no like learn laidis.  I like go back Hawai'i.

We wen stay in da room
wit my madda holding me
listening to da news
waiting fo hear about da President.

## Intermediate School

Everybody from all da elementary schools
suppose to go to da same intermediate school,
so I see pleny kids I dunno.
Everybody checking each odda out.
Get pleny buildings and one big cafeteria.
Dis school been around fo long time
so get leaks in da ceiling wen rain
and pleny windows get wood on top
cuz da glass underneath stay broken.
Every time no mo toilet pepa in da girls' room.
No mo nuff books fo everybody so everybody gotta share.
Some books get any kine writing inside and get some pages stay rip
      out.
I told my madda da books look old, and she ask me if I like change
      school.
I no like make hassle fo change school.  Gotta get district acceptance
or someting laidat so I tell her I can handle.

Next to da school get one gas station and one small store
where you can buy any kine stuffs like soda and chips.
Get pleny people dea so my madda told me fo wait fo her
in front da store by da big store window.
As wea she going pick me up.

Wen da last bell wen ring,
I wen walk wit my classmate to da store.
As wea her madda was going pick her up too.
Her madda wen come first fo pick her up
and I was going walk in front da big store window like my madda
      said
but I was waving bye to my classmate and I neva like be rude.

Afta da car wen drive away, den I wen walk
and one group of kids wen surround me and ask me fo quarta.
I told um I no mo quarta, dey take my backpack but,
and dey wen find all my dolla bills.
Dey wen grab all da money and shove da backpack to me.

Right wen dey wen go, my madda wen come wit da car.
I was crying so much dat I no can talk wen my madda wen ask me
    wat wen happen.

Wen we got home, I pau cry
but I still neva like tell my madda wat wen happen.
I suppose to wait fo her in front da window and I neva.
She keep asking but I no answer.
Den come dark and I suppose to throw away da rubbish outside da
    house.
I know I no can go outside wen dark.  You no can see nobody.

How I suppose to go outside?
My body wen get all sweaty and hot.
So I finally tell my madda wat wen happen.
She was so mad, but I no rememba who wen take da money.
Even if I rememba, you tink I going tell on dem?
Shoot, I wish I wen tell my madda fo change school,
den, I can still go out wen dark.
But I neva, so I gotta throw da rubbish away daytime.

People tell me dat dis suppose to be da best time of my life.
If das da case, everyting else going be crap
and my best time was in elementary school.
Dey betta be wrong, man
cuz I no can live like dis.

## I Wen Lose Me

Da school year was hard,
and I was looking forward to da break.
Maybe da break was too good but.
Wen I came back to school,
I dunno wat wen really happen.
Was like I wen get lost
in Septemba.

I neva fit in.
I dunno was weird.
I was super sensitive to everyting.
Was just like da story you hear on da news
wen somebody wake up from one coma
and gotta learn how fo do everyting again.
No get me wrong, I can walk,
but I wen forget how I walk.
You know, how everybody
get dea own stride.

As hard.
People keep asking me why I walk funny.
Dey tell me dat I should walk regular,
but I forget how.
I start getting all sweaty
feel like I losing it.

I no talk pleny like I used to befo.
I dunno wat fo say
and how fo say um.
I tink I wen lose me.

I keep looking myself
in da mirror.
Da longa I look my hands
da mo I can see all
da little veins.
I feel like I dissolving.

My madda ask me if I ok.
I no feel good but.
I dunno how fo explain how I feel.
She tell me if I like see one docta,
and I tell her I dunno.

I tell her my body no feel sick.
I just feel nervous and I dunno why.
I no tink one docta can help me.
Den she tell me she talking about
one different kine docta.

I wen get mo hot.
I tink I ok.
I get mad at her
and ask her wat kine docta
she tink I need.
She no answer.  Den I know
wat kine docta she talking about.

I ask her if she really tink
I need dat kine docta.
Den she ask me how I feel again.
I go to my room and look at da mirror again.
I dunno wat stay happening.
I just like go back to how I was befo.
I look my face, and I not smiling.
I look different.
I try not fo sweat.
I keep repeating my name ova and ova.
Weird but hearing my name make me feel betta.

If I keep telling my name maybe
I going feel da way I suppose to feel.
I going fit in wit everybody.
I no need one da kine docta.
Everyting going be ok.

## Making Makizushi

"How come you no talk?"
My bachan look at me and smile.
She put da bamboo mat out fo roll
sushi fo New Year.
"Go roll sushi."
She give me one sheet nori
and put um on da mat.
Den she show me how fo spread da rice on da nori.
"Ova hea no put rice."
So I spread da rice on most of da nori
and leave da rest of da nori witout rice.
Den I follow her.
I put red sprinkle in one row across da rice.
Den I put da tuna, carrot, watacress, mushroom, and kampyo.
Den she help me roll da sushi.
Afta my bachan, madda, and me wen finish roll
all da sushi and pau wash da dishes,
my madda wrap some sushi in wax pepa
fo give some people.

We had pleny roll sushi,
and we was going have tempura,
soba, ozoni, and special kine food laidat.
Da house was clean and was nice fo
help get ready fo New Year.

My madda wen rub my head
wen she pass by.
Feel so good fo be wit everybody.
I wish winta break could last foreva.
I like everyday be like today
all busy and warm.

# Japan Trip

My family been hea long time.
I no rememba wen dey wen leave Japan.
We been hea in Hawai'i befo statehood—
my bachan wanted us fo visit Japan but,
cuz I neva been dea befo and she wen like
introduce me to da family.

Was one long trip and my body all tired
cuz I stay jetlag.
We visit all da tourist kine place.
I dunno wat dey tink of me.
Dey come up to me and start talking Japanese
den I gotta tell dem wakarimasen.
I no undastand wat dey talking das why.

Remind me of wen I go Waikīkī.
People extra nice to me like dey going sell me someting.
Den wen I open my mouth, dey know I not from Japan
so dey go away.
Eh, maybe I get money, maybe I like buy someting.
Watevas.

We wen go visit my family in da country.
At da house, my bachan wen drop to da floor
and bow so low I neva know wat fo do.
I just standing on da side in my jeans and I feel so stupid.
I no like insult nobody and I dunno wat fo do.
My bachan start talking Japanese and I dunno wat she talking.

Mo betta if I wen pay mo attention afta elementary school
wen I used to go to da Hongwanji mission fo learn Japanese.
Hard fo study Japanese but, wen you like be like everybody else
and nobody talking Japanese.

Look like my bachan explaining someting.
Everybody stay nodding and smiling at me.
Ho, good ting man.

Weird, yeah.  I know how fo be in my house
but I dunno wat fo do hea.

Sometime hard fo be Local.
Sometime hard fo be American.
And sometime hard fo be Japanese.

Sometime I feel like I no belong no place.
I wonda if people tink befo dey come stay Hawai'i.
Hawai'i good but I know I wen lose someting.
Hard fo go back.

# Hiroshima

We wen visit da museum and had all kine pikchas on top da walls.
I no rememba if was one real pikcha or one painting,
but I rememba had one lady and her breast wen melt.
I wen ask my sista if she tink people really melt laidat
or disappear fast like in da movie *The Day After*.
She neva answer.  I guess she dunno.

She wen ask me if I tink get radiation ova hea.
I look at all da people in da museum.  Was pack.
I told her I no tink get radiation
cuz get pleny tourist.
Layda on, my sista wen get upset stomach, and
she keep asking me if I tink get radiation.

I wonda if she was sick fo real.
You know she wen see all da pikchas
and hard fo see dat kine stuff.
Hard fo forget.
Maybe das why we wen go.

## Pearl Harbor

One day, I was near Pearl Harbor, and I saw some planes flying low.
The planes flew so low that I could see a red circle under one of the planes.
I forgot they were filming the movie *Pearl Harbor* today.

I hear a boom and see gray smoke.

Many people of Japanese ancestry fought for America.
The government sent apology letters for Americans interned during the war.
It is hard to live when Americans do not treat you as an American.

## Obon Dance

I don't understand what they say at the ceremony,
but I say a prayer for everyone who passed away.
I tell my bachan and jichan that everything is all right,
and I hope they are fine.

I go outside to dance in happi coat and jeans.
I don't understand any of the songs because the songs are in Japanese,
but I follow the person in front of me and dance in the circle.

It is a good feeling like I'm a part of a bigger family.
When we go home, the ride is so smooth.  I can sleep deeply.

# Japanese 102

I learning kanji.  Ho, kanji so hard.
Get so much strokes fo write one kanji character.
Da orda and direction fo each stroke important too.
I not used to tinking laidis.
I used to alphabets.

Den get all kine way fo talk to people.
Get honorific, polite, and casual.
Get different way fo count stuff
depend on wat you counting.
Man, I getting hard time.

One day, we suppose to talk to one guest speaka.
I wen ask one question, but she neva undastand wat I saying.
I bet I stay talking Japanese like one foreigner.
I get all hot and red.
I no like insult her but I getting da
honorific, polite, casual talk all mix up.
I no like talk already, but I haftu cuz I still stay in class
and everybody waiting.

Ho, dis class so hard.
I shame.  I Japanese
and I feel like I suppose to know
how fo talk Japanese.
Hard fo learn but.

# Tea Ceremony in Hawai'i

Shoji doors were open
so I walked down the gray stone path
to watch a tea ceremony.

No one dressed in kimono.
All the women wore jeans and socks.
Today was for practice.

I removed my shoes and entered.
I sat on tatami mats to watch
women learn how to walk into a room,
rinse a cup, pour, use a chasen
to mix matcha and water.

Every movement was observed and corrected.

When practice ended, everyone moved to another room.
I thanked them and was about to leave
when a woman brought a small tray of cookies.

I quickly kneeled and followed her,
chose the cookie closest to me,
and placed it on the paper provided.

She put a cup of matcha in my hand.
I turned the cup clockwise twice.

I slowly drank
every drop of matcha
every fiber of tatami
every square of shoji.

I thanked the woman again, exited,
put on my running shoes,
and walked away from the stone path
toward the grass and went back home.

## Stereotype

I no like be da stereotype Japanese teacha
who no like undastand da local student
or da high maka maka Japanese manager
who expect everybody fo work extra hard
or da overachievas who tink dey mo betta than everybody else.
As not me, man.

Even get da Asian women stereotype.
Like dey suppose to be all exotic and submissive.
I neva know dat some guys like Asian women
until I wen go on one plane to da mainland
and had some guys talking to me like I no undastand English.
No can be my Pidgin. I neva say nothing yet.
Dey talk slow and smile pleny
like dey flirting with me or someting.
Dey so much older than me.
Someting wrong wit dem.
Dey tell me how dey was going meet some women
but it neva work out.
Yeah, like dey really get chance with me.
Forget it.
I was looking outside da window,
and dey no catch da hint dat I no like talk to dem.
So dey talk and talk and talk.
Wen dinner came, one of da guys wen hold one bun up to my face
like I neva see one dinner roll befo. Get real.
Afta dinner, I wen put da blanket ova my head
and my friend next to me wen do da same ting too.
Must be we wen shock da guys. I wen hea some gasping
wen we was unda da blankets.
Eh, maybe we going start one new stereotype.
Asian women who like go sleep wit blankets ova dea heads.

# Mānoa Stream: 2006

For three weeks from my dorm I heard
the stream and thunder.  Today, the rain stopped.
I had to visit the stream.  The water is calmer,
but I can still hear it.

I like the stream because it belongs.
This stream must have been here
before the koi pond, guava trees, and houses.

My family has been here in Hawai'i for a long time—
no one asks why the stream is here.
The stream is lucky.

I watch the water pass the rocks flowing forever
and stay until I have to go back.
I listen to the stream from my window
and lie here.

## No Can Sleep

I no can sleep, so I start writing.
I write about any kine stuffs.
Sometimes I no can sleep, and I no can write.
I just stare at da ceiling.
My head feel so heavy, but
I no can let go and go back sleep.
Wen dis happen hard fo function next day.
Even hard fo take nap.
Gunfunit, I gotta get some sleep.

I wen talk to my friend,
and she tell me no drink so much coffee.
I tell her I neva drink coffee last night.
I just no can sleep.  Maybe I tinking too much.
Maybe I worry too much,
but not like I get stuff fo worry about.
Everyting ok so far.
She ask me wat I tinking about,
and I tell her I always tinking about writing.
Den she say no worry about writing.
I ask her wat if I no mo nothing else fo say?
Wat if I dry up and no can write?
She look at me and tell me,
No worry.  You always going get someting fo say.
Da world not dat good.

~Rememba Wen~

## Ogo Picking

My madda wen tell me we was going 'Ewa Beach fo pick ogo.
Weneva we pick ogo, we have one picnic too.
My fadda put all da hibachi and food inside da car and we go 'Ewa.
Long ride and on each side of da road, all cane fields.

Afta he wen start da fire fo da hibachi,
he wen cook da spare ribs my madda wen soak
in one shoyu ginger sauce da night befo.
Was so ono eating everyting unda da tree.

We wen rest little while.  Den, we all go in da ocean.
My madda tell me fo look fo da brown ogo.
She show me one ogo dat wen float by us and
tell me if da ogo stay connected to someting
I suppose to break off da top so da ogo can grow some mo.

Had pleny ogo.
We was on da shallow side, but one wave was coming,
and I neva know cuz my back was to da ocean.
My sista wen try fo warn me but was too late.
Da wave wen go ova me.
All I see is ocean, sand, ogo, and my air bubbles going up.

Fo couple seconds was real quiet unda da wata.
Sound weird but was peaceful until I came out.
My eyes wen sting, and I was coughing up wata.
Afta dat time, I no turn my back to da ocean.

Da next day, my madda wen make da ogo
wit onion, rice vinega, shoyu, and suga.
Was so ono fo eat, and I like da ogo crunch.

We still cook outside on da hibachi,
but we neva pick ogo long time.
Now days, no mo too much ogo.
Just get pleny houses 'Ewa side.

## Me and My Sista

I wen ask my sista if she like ride on my tricycle.
Me and her at da same time.  Good fun dat kine.

She neva like cuz everybody in our family
tell us no ride laidat befo somebody get hurt.
I told her going be ok, no worry.
So me and her wen ride da same time.
Was fun til she wen fall down
and scrape her knee on da cement by da garage.

Da blood was coming out.  She stay crying so much,
I wen panic.  I help her off da cement.
She still crying so I pretend
I was one of da paramedics from *Emergency!*
"Rrrrr, Emergency! Emergency!"
I take her to our bachan's room
and clean da scrape.

Den I turn on da TV so she can watch cartoon.
She wen stop crying, so I wen ask her if she like drink juice
and I wen bring her da juice.  She ok now.

I no can stand wen she cry,
especially wen she believe me
wen I tell her nothing bad going happen.

# Bowling

Afta we wen go bowling fo P.E.,
I saw my classmate eat eight slices pizza at Pizza Hut.
Everybody wen cheer her on.
I wish I can eat eight slices too,
but I can only eat four max.

Da next time we wen go bowling,
da same girl wen eat only two slices.
She said she was so full,
and she no can eat even one mo slice.
Eh, she lying. I dunno why she ack laidat.
I know she can eat eight slices.

Den, I notice all da girls ack different.
Dey no play outside. All day, dey talk story
scoping out da boys.
Had one girl everybody was scared of.
She can beat everybody up
even da boys.
Now, she wear makeup and lipstick
trying fo be dainty.
Nobody say nothing—
she can still pound you.

I dunno wat wen happen,
but da rules wen change.
Now, da pretty girls get all da attention.

Da one, who like fit in, wen change.
Da one, who no change,
get left out on da side.

## Prom Night

We wen dance all da slow dance.
I put my hands on his shoulders,
and he put his hands on my waist.
Was so nice fo dance wit him.
We wen dance all da songs by
Whitney Houston and Peter Cetera.

I wen move my hands little bit closer to his neck,
and he wen move his hands little bit mo around my waist.
We wen keep inching around each odda
until we wen hold each odda.
I put my chin on his shoulder,
and he put his chin on mine.
I wen close my eyes, and we was swaying
song afta song.

He wen even hold my hand layda on dat night.
We wen walk outside fo little while.
Was so nice.

Den, was time fo go.  We neva have one limo
and he neva have his license yet
so my parents wen pick us up.

We wen go his house fo drop him off.
He wanted fo kiss me
but my madda wen turn around fo tell him bye
so he wen kiss me on da cheek real fast kine
and dig out.

Da kiss was nice, but I wish my madda neva turn around.
As wat happen wen you get one chaperone afta da prom.

~Wen Nobody Stay Looking~

## Dancing Wit One Molesta

I was at my friend's party
and all her family and friends was dea.
I dunno why I wen go da party.
Only a few days ago she wen tell me
dat somebody in da family was touching her.
You know, da way not suppose to touch.
Den she tell me he said he not going touch her
laidat no mo and everyting going be ok.
Was one big secret and she told me not fo tell nobody.
She my friend so I neva tell nobody
but at da party, I saw da guy.
Ho da weird, everybody stay laughing and smiling
like nothing.
Afta everybody pau eat, dey wen put on da music.
Had some fast songs and everybody was dancing
den dey wen play da slow songs.
You know, da boy-girl kine songs.

I was sitting down wen da guy wen ask me fo dance.
I neva like go dance wit him.  He old and I know wat he was doing
    to my friend.
Everybody smiling and telling me fo go dance.
My friend wen look at me, and she pretend like everyting ok.
I neva like dance, but everybody look at me funny kine way.
Why I no dance wit him?
So, I wen stand up and dance wit him.
I dunno how fo dance slow dance, but he said
das ok cuz he going teach me how.
He told me dat if his body move one way,
I gotta move my body da odda way.
We wen dance little while den I told him I tired.
He said I doing ok and wanted fo dance some mo.
I told him sorry, and walk away.

I wen tell my friend I wanted fo go home already,
and I like use her phone fo call my parents fo pick me up.
She give me da phone and ask me if I going tell anybody.
I told her I going tell my parents.  Everyting so weird.

Den she grab my arm and say I betta not tell nobody.
As one secret and everyting ok now.
She tell me I going mess everyting up.

My madda wen answer da phone and dat she going pick me up.
I neva tell my madda wat wen happen yet but I told my friend I was
    going tell her.
My friend was so mad at me dat she neva notice I was sweating.
I dunno how she can live laidis.
I no can believe I wen dance wit him
and everybody stay smiling.

# Bumping on da Bus

Rememba we was going home on da bus?
Da time had one guy standing up next to me
and you and me had one seat?
Sure, you rememba.
Was weird, yeah?

Da bus was full so everybody was pack,
and we was on our way home from college.
We was young yet, maybe only nineteen or twenty.
Had da guy dat kept bumping me on my shoulder.
Everytime he bump me, I go look to da right and see his pants.
Eh, no can help.
Wen somebody bump you
das wat you do.
He keep bumping me on my shoulder
until da lady behind me
wen tell him fo stop.

He look all innocent at da lady
like he dunno wat he was doing.
Den da lady tell him,
"You know wat you was doing."
He must have been doing someting wrong.
He wen stop bumping me.

Sometimes, I tink about dat, you know.
Was real funny kine.
Layda, had one class talking about people lidat.
Da guest speaka was talking about sex crimes and any kine stuff.
Scary, yeah.
Was in front everybody too.
I no like tink wat kine stuff people do
wen nobody stay looking.

# Garbage

Her head is too heavy so she puts her fingers around her eyes to remove them. Then she inserts her fingers into the empty eye sockets and attempts to dislocate her head from her neck. After some effort, she places her head next to the dishes. Her neck feels better and she washes dishes until the rack is filled. Then she lies down on the table and waits for her husband.

He walks in and asks for a knife, but the body does not move. After three minutes, he opens a drawer and pulls out a large knife. He walks to the body on the table and slices its breasts off, throws away innards, and washes the hollow organs. Then he opens a can of soup and empties it into one of the breasts. He pours coffee into the other breast. When he's finished eating, he stands, rubs his stomach, and looks at the empty containers and the body. He folds the body in half so the neck touches the knees. Then he bends the knees so the ankles touch the ass. He throws the body and empty breasts into a plastic bag for collection tomorrow. Then he washes the soup can, dries it with a dish towel, and places the can in a box. Ready for delivery to a nearby recycling center on Friday.

# Red Velvet Cake

A frying pan forced her husband to sleep. She slowly dragged his body below the wooden floor sliding him over the stairs into the basement for her unplanned party for one.

Tonight, he was her red velvet cake. The surprises continued from the cloth around his wrists attached to a nearby pole, tie-dyed in blood, to a shiny knife that cuts skin. His eyes opened. They were narrow at first then his eyes were big cherries. His voice pierced the ceiling and floated to the CD player in the living room. She always wanted to direct an opera, and today was her debut. She cut her cake until all she heard was his favorite music.

When she walked up the stairs, she could hear sirens. It was obvious the whole neighborhood heard. She wondered where everyone was when she was screaming there.

## Repulsive Love

after you manipulate a thousand languages
my scream boils into a whisper

you beat delicate wills
and smear me with mad lust
ugly licks and heaves

you worship a delirious dream of repulsive love
a woman is an apparatus
a raw breast
a shadow

my frantic sleep never stops
i need to storm away
take wind through music
and love like a girl

-Mortality-

.

# Feva

I was trying fo do my homework,
was hard fo concentrate, but.
I had one feva and one head cold.
Must have been going around
cuz my friend told me
get pleny students stay out sick.

I was getting dizzy, so I wen walk back to bed.
Befo I wen lie down, I pass my window
and saw da red ginger by da grass.
So nice. Ho, my head floating.
Man, would be nice if I can float
out da window fo pick up some red ginger, yeah?

I gotta sit down. Wen you sick, easy fo notice any kine stuff.
Like all da pukas in da screen window.
I wen even find one termite stay trapped inside da screen.
Poor ting, yeah? No mo wings. Look like one worm
just trying fo get in and nobody wen notice.
Nobody care about one termite.
Sad yeah, if nobody care about wat happen to you.
Den, you gotta take care yourself.
Lucky ting I get family.

I lie down and look at da ceiling.
Wat if I neva have one family?
I know some people no mo family
and life hard fo dem.
Lucky ting everybody still get dea healt.
Lucky ting all I get is one feva and head cold.
I close my eyes and da dizziness go away
and I fall into one deep sleep.

# Modest Inquisition

Why do I look through a water ceiling
to break my teaspoons of air?
Why do I plan my red eruption?
When did I fill a joy bag with pills?
Am I tired of writing my pain poems?

Was it the polite mirage?
The incomplete painting?
The glass boxes of water?
Is that why I want to break?

I deal with impossible time.
Stop sitting in my blue chair.
Throw away my joy bag.
This is not the day I say goodbye.

## Plumeria

I watch the plumeria tree from my glass window.
The tree is covered with white yellow flowers.

I know the tree could not hold me
if I were to fall from my building window.

The branches would splinter
and I would be covered with flowers.

My body would be resting on the ground
among the scent of plumeria, blood, and milk.

I look at the sky.
A perfect sunny day.

## Eternal Love

The shelters
are too busy
to see us
on the sidewalk.

The streets are
empty
and your heart
beats slower.

I wait.
Your heart
stops.

I lie still
beside you
welcoming
death.

## Mortality

walk and dirt licks red
rain and digests hair skin so I
run to the house near the plumeria tree
ti leaf plant pull break tear and shake
their leaves into silver threads the
ground is ebony
chords and I stand
on rooftops until chairs
burn and sink every
limb wire pole I will be
time I will be
foot and strength
sifted away

# On the Way Home

The day was quiet
except for the wind.

She kept walking
watching the tree
branches in the sun.

She did not know
she was dead.

She ran through
the weeds
and water walls.

Kissing forget-me-nots
on the way home.

# Biopsy

After one normal and two abnormal test results,
the doctor told me that a biopsy was required,
so I walked into one of the rooms.
The nurse showed me the swabs,
liquids, and wrapped tools that would be used.
Although I could not see the tools,
she said they look like little scissors
and the doctor will clip a small piece of tissue
out and the sample will be examined.
I will know the results in three days.
I asked if it could be cancer,
and she replied
it was highly unlikely.
I lay down and the doctor came in.
I had no other questions.

# Dead Dreams

A wooden soldier walks
his chest covered in blood
and I am frozen.

I am not afraid of the soldier
or of the blood.

It is the smiling child next to him.
The child is not crying
or running.

The child is dead.
Then I realize

I am the child.

I wake up
not wanting to know
the meaning of dreams.

My heart screams.

# Time

It was a happy time
covered in broken
glass and numbers.

We stayed inside
listening to rain
and hearing our breaths.

Then, there was a ticking
from the wall
past the hands
through the ring.

Who knew it would end so quickly?
The momentary ticks.
Holding our breaths
until there was no time left.

# River

The river is flooded.
After the heavy rains of October,
the leaves traverse the overflow
and I watch with my eyes wide.

After the heavy rains of October,
you turned to ash
and I watch with my eyes wide
as you float above me.

You turned to ash.
I walk into the river
as you float above me.
My tissue becomes translucent.

I walk into the river.
My body is light.
My tissue becomes translucent
as I breathe cold water.

My body is light
when I see your face.
As I breathe cold water,
I hold your unexpected hand.

When I see your face,
I follow you.
I hold your unexpected hand
and feel the pain of air.

I follow you
out of the river
and feel the pain of air.
I reach for the bank.

Out of the river,
the leaves traverse the overflow.
I reach for the bank.
The river is flooded.

# After 9/11

News was constant.  Everyone was on alert.
There was a sad feeling like nothing was going to get better.
The government told everyone to continue working.
It was hard to do anything.

The economy wasn't good, and many people stayed home.
I had to watch movies on videotape and some comedies.
I even watched the shopping channels on cable.
People were watching so many movies that households
replaced their VHS players with DVD players.

It was comforting to look at the flag.
So many people bought flags that some stores ran out.
I played *The Star Spangled Banner, God Bless America,* and *God
    Bless the U.S.A.*
and appreciated the voices of Whitney Houston, Celine Dion, and
    Lee Greenwood.

Everyone just wanted everything to get better.
I wanted everyone to heal, so I could look back
and wonder how we survived this.

~Outside~

## Walks with Bachan

Shower trees with circles of yellow and pink
remind me of primavera flowers near home.

I walked with my bachan
to Times and Cornet in the morning.
She showed me flowers as we passed each yard.
Plumeria, pikake, gardenia,
red ginger, hibiscus, and orchid.

When she passed away, she deserved more than mums.
I picked every bird-of-paradise, white ginger, and anthurium from
    our garden.

## Roses

When I sleep, I dream
I am alone in empty fields.
Men have gone and tools have been returned.
Sheltered from light rain,
I remain looking at cut roses.
Perfect roses that will be sold,
and lesser roses that will be discarded.
My hands dig into soil.
I remove and hide roses.
The roses will be safe
in my garden behind the weeds.

## Taking Pictures

By the time I found my camera, it was too late.
The bird flew away, so I waited a little while.
I walked around and looked up in the trees.
Then, I heard a long whistle.  So pretty.

It is easy to forget everything here.
Only trees, birds, and quiet.

It was getting dark, so I inhaled clean air
and walked back to the pavement.

## Zebra Dove

I never saw a dove lie
so flat on the cement floor
checking its feathers
in the sun

extending a wing
all the way
to the other side

feathers
underneath
exposed

then lie tilted
unnoticed
as students passed by.

After three minutes,
the dove stood up,
and I saw a limb
with no toes.

The zebra dove trusts
and lives.

I close my eyes
wanting to dissolve
myself into everything.

## About the Author

Ann Inoshita was born and raised on Oʻahu. She has been published in *Bamboo Ridge: Journal of Hawaiʻi Literature and Arts, Hawaiʻi Pacific Review,* and has other publications forthcoming. She is in the M.A. program in English with a Creative Writing concentration at the University of Hawaiʻi at Mānoa. She is a 2006 recipient of the Myrle Clark Award for Creative Writing and a 2007 recipient of The John Young Scholarship in the Arts. This is her first book of poems.

Made in the USA
Middletown, DE
10 September 2023

37655999R00047